NATIONAL GEOGRAPHIC

Ladders

EMPIRE STATE BUILDING

AMERICAN WONDERS

GENRE History Article Read to find out about the Empire State Building.

THE EIGHTH WONDER OF THE WORLD

by Hugh Westrup

Imagine yourself perched on a narrow steel beam high above New York City. In your hands you hold a powerful rivet gun, a tool used for building. You duck as a large beam swings through the air overhead. You have no hard hat to protect your head and no safety ropes to keep you from falling. It's more than a thousand-foot drop to the street below.

Workers had faced highly dangerous jobs before 1930. But this job was especially risky: constructing the world's tallest **skyscraper** of its time. A skyscraper is a very tall building, so tall that it seems to "scrape" the sky.

Two New Yorkers, Al Smith and John Jakob Raskob, dreamed of constructing this **landmark**. Smith was a former governor of the state of New York and Raskob was a wealthy businessman. In a short period of time, these two important men managed to plan, get money for, and start construction on a giant building at the corner of Fifth Avenue and Thirty-Fourth Street, in the heart of New York City.

A SKYSCRAPER IS SO TALL THAT IT SEEMS TO "SCRAPE" THE SKY.

People called the Empire State Building the "eighth wonder of the world." Why? It was taller than any human-made structure on Earth.

A DARING DEED

The 1920s was a time of growth and riches in the United States. In New York City, one skyscraper after another went up, each taller than the one before. By 1930, the tallest skyscraper in New York was the sleek Chrysler Building, owned by the Chrysler auto company. But it wouldn't be the tallest skyscraper for long.

John Jakob Raskob had once been one of the bosses at General Motors, one of Chrysler's rivals. Raskob didn't want to be outdone by Chrysler. His skyscraper would reach even higher than the Chrysler Building. He would name it the Empire State Building, after one of the nicknames of the state of New York: the Empire State. This nickname celebrated the state's importance in business and culture in the country and in the world.

Raskob and Smith moved quickly on their plan, and it was a good thing they did. As the project began in 1930, the economy was in a downfall. Businesses closed, banks failed, and millions of Americans lost their jobs and their savings. It was a tough time financially across the country. So began the **Great Depression**, one of the grimmest eras in American history.

But the construction of the Empire State Building continued. It was a risky project for its 3,400-worker construction crew. Many of them would be working higher off the ground than they ever had before. They needed courage and steady nerves. There was often no safety equipment to protect steelworkers against falls. Still, the project offered workers a steady paycheck in desperate economic times.

This brave, steady worker waves for the camera high above the city.

This is a view of the Empire State Building during construction. You can see the steel frame at the top. It took about 57,000 tons of steel to build the frame.

THE BEST SHOW IN TOWN

Crowds of people gathered every day to watch the construction of the Empire State Building. The show's stars were the workers who assembled the building's steel skeleton—workers with titles such as riveter, connector, and ground crew workers, each with a different skill.

These workers needed more than bravery and a willingness to do hard work. They needed special skills.

GROUND CREW A ground crew worker used a power drill to break up rock at the building site. After ground workers removed all the rock, they built the structure's foundation, or base.

CONNECTOR A connector climbed up and down the columns. He grabbed heavy steel beams that swung from cranes. He pushed the beams into place. That got them ready for the riveters.

RIVETER A rivet is a bolt used to connect two steel beams. One riveter used metal tongs to toss a red-hot rivet to the catcher. The catcher then caught the hot rivet in a can. The catcher put the rivet into a hole in the beam. Then another worker used a noisy rivet gun to fuse it into the steel. Fusing the rivet locked the beam in place next to another beam.

SKYWALKING

Not many people have what it takes to walk across steel beams hundreds of feet high in blustery winds every day. This skill is called *skywalking*. Many skywalkers are Native Americans belonging to the Mohawk tribe. The Mohawk have helped build some of the tallest skyscrapers in the United States, including the Empire State Building. They've also enjoyed lunch high in the sky, as shown in the photo below.

The Mohawk first began skywalking in the mid-1880s, when some Mohawk were helping to build a bridge near the tribe's Canadian reservation. Though their job was to unload supplies, Mohawk men eventually started climbing the bridge to see what other workers were doing. Managers noticed that the Mohawk workers showed amazing steadiness on the bridge and had little fear of heights. Soon, managers hired the Mohawk to work high in the air—and they're still at it today.

TOPPING IT OFF

The Empire State Building was originally going to be 1,050 feet tall—two feet higher than its nearby rival, the Chrysler Building. Then Al Smith hit on the idea of adding a 200-foot tower. Visitors could ride an elevator from an observation deck on the 86th floor to an even higher floor at the top of the tower.

A grander view wasn't the main purpose of the tower, though. Smith hoped the tower would be a docking station. In the 1920s, people thought that the aircraft of the future was the dirigible. A dirigible is a large, propeller-driven aircraft. It contains a large chamber that is filled with gases that are lighter than the air around it. This causes the dirigible to rise, like a balloon filled with helium. Many people believed that dirigibles would be more popular than airplanes as a form of transportation for people and goods.

Smith wanted the Empire State Building's tower to be designed so a balloon-like dirigible could be connected to it. A dirigible arriving from London or Paris would "park" at the top of the tower. Passengers would take a stairway to the observation deck and take the elevator from there to ground level.

Smith's dirigible scheme never worked out. The winds at the top of the building are too powerful for a dirigible to dock. They blow in several directions at once. A dirigible connected to the tower would bob around like a toy balloon. It was just as well. The dirigible never really caught on as a form of transportation.

This illustration shows what a dirigible would have looked like approaching the docking station on the Empire State Building.

Workers "top off" the grand skyscraper with a tower that is 200 feet tall.

LIGHTING UP THE SKY

The Empire State Building opened on May 1, 1931. Two of Al Smith's grandchildren cut the ceremonial ribbon. Cutting a ceremonial ribbon is a way that many people celebrate the opening of a new building or business. Minutes later, President Herbert Hoover pushed a button in the White House, about 225 miles away, to turn on the lights of the Empire State Building.

"The House That Smith Built," as one newspaper called it, was an immediate sensation. It quickly passed the Statue of Liberty to become New York's most popular tourist attraction. A total of 775,000 visitors rode elevators up to the observation decks in the first year. All Americans, especially New Yorkers, looked up at it with pride. The city came together to build the tallest building in a record amount of time, even during hard times. Later in 1931, the designer of the Empire State Building, William F. Lamb, received the Gold Medal from the New York Architectural League for his beautiful design.

Today, there are at least 20 skyscrapers taller than the Empire State Building. Still, the Empire State Building is as popular as ever, with about four million people visiting it every year.

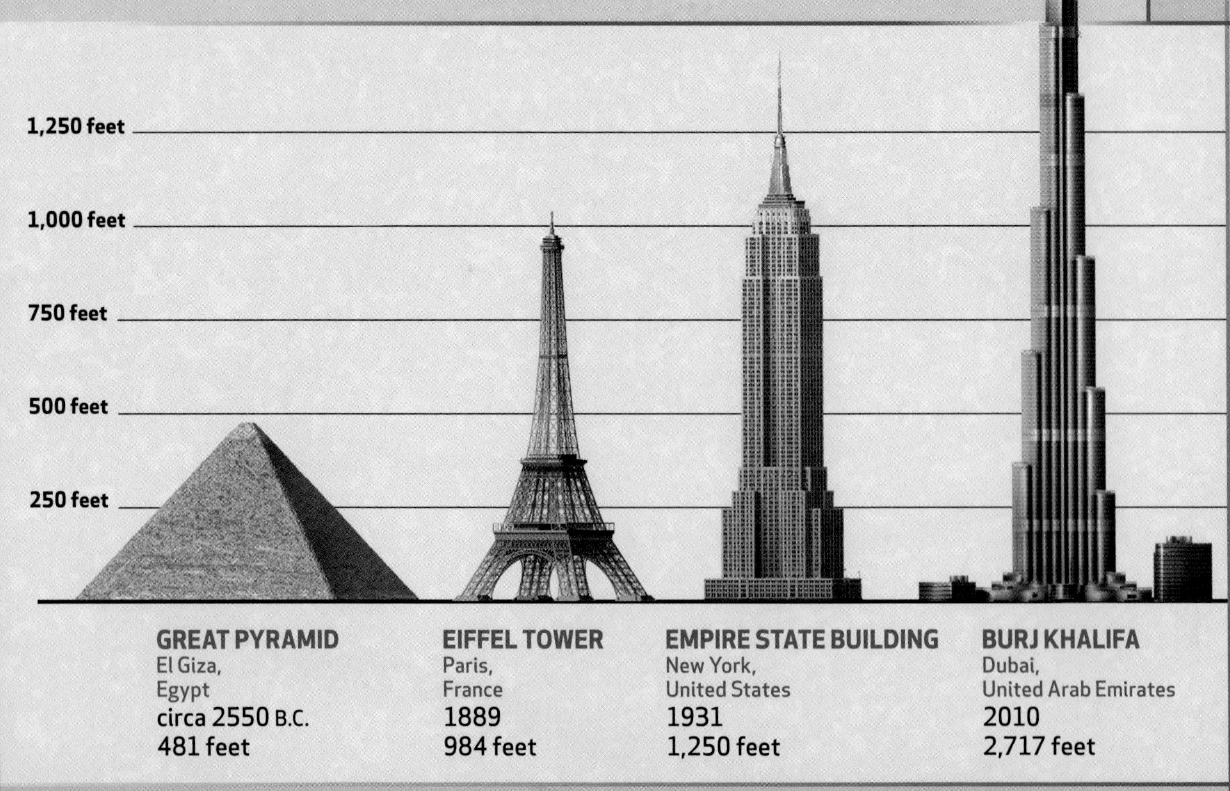

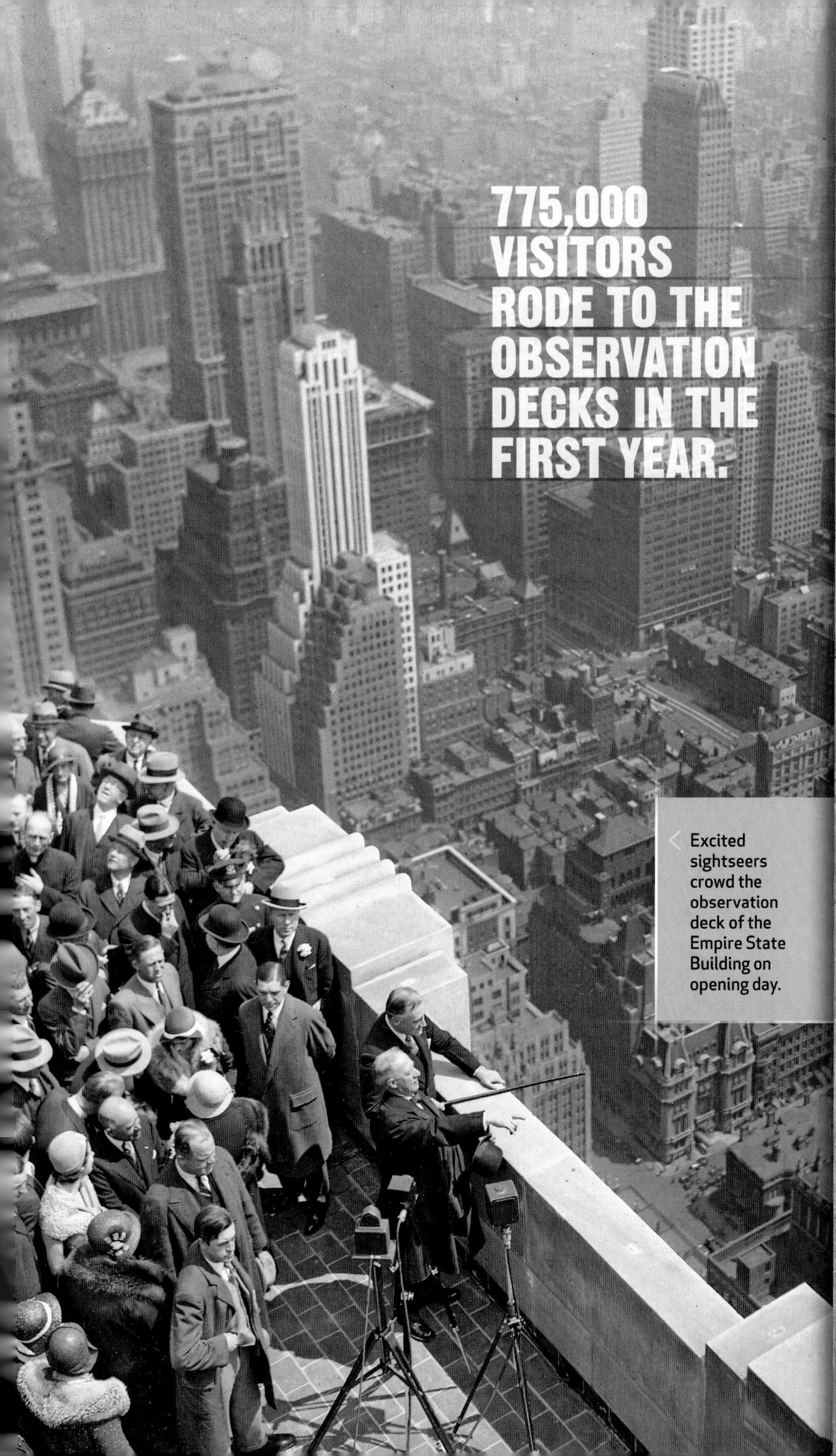

775,000 VISITORS RODE TO THE OBSERVATION DECKS IN THE FIRST YEAR.

Excited sightseers crowd the observation deck of the Empire State Building on opening day.

IN GOOD CONDITION

Just as you care for something of value, a team of people makes sure the Empire State Building, one of New York City's greatest landmarks, is kept clean and in good working order. The elevators need to work, the lobby and all 102 floors need to shine, and every one of the building's more than 6,500 windows needs a good washing.

Can you imagine trying to keep all of the Empire State Building's windows clean? It's a monumental chore, and it never ends! Every day, workers hang from the outside walls like Spider-Man, washing windows. According to one experienced window washer, it would take three workers four months to wash every window in the building. Once they're done, it's time to start over again. If four months seems like a long time, imagine what it would be like if there was only one person washing all those windows. It would take that window washer about a year to wash every one of the Empire State Building's windows.

This worker is on the Empire State Building's tower. He is changing a lightbulb in the tower's beacon light. The light glows to mark the top of the building so airplane pilots know to avoid it.

EMPIRE STATE BUILDING BY THE NUMBERS

- **60,000** TONS OF STEEL
- **200,000** CUBIC FEET OF LIMESTONE AND GRANITE
- **10** MILLION BRICKS
- **730** TONS OF ALUMINUM AND STAINLESS STEEL
- MORE THAN **6,500** WINDOWS

Window washers were called "sparrows." They got that name because of the way they perched on the windowsills. Only their toes and a leather safety belt held them in place.

Check In How did building the Empire State Building help the people of New York City during the Great Depression?

Read to find out how elevators changed buildings.

GOING UP!

by Elizabeth Massie

The ten-story Home Insurance Building in Chicago wasn't exactly gigantic by today's standards, but when it was built in 1885, it was the world's first skyscraper. Inspired by its height, builders quickly began constructing taller and taller buildings. What allowed them to build such tall structures? One thing was the development of better and safer elevators, since few people could climb all the stairs to the top of a skyscraper.

In the mid-1800s, simple elevators were used to move goods between floors in factories. But people did not ride in them. The cables , or metal ropes, that lifted and lowered an elevator could break, and the elevator could come crashing down. For that reason, people were afraid to ride in them.

In 1852, Elisha Otis changed everything. He invented a brake to stop an elevator from falling if its cable broke. Otis demonstrated his elevator brake at an 1854 **exposition**, or public show. He stood inside one of his elevators. Another man cut the elevator cable with an axe. The elevator only fell a few inches before the brake stopped it. Otis's invention led to the development of safe elevators that people weren't afraid to ride. After that, builders could construct buildings that were taller than ever before, since nobody had to climb the stairs. The Woolworth Building (1913) towered at 60 stories tall. The Empire State Building (1931) reached 102 stories.

Elisha Otis's company installed the elevators in the Empire State Building.

This magnificent elevator is in the Essex House Hotel in New York City.

FROM THE GROUND UP

There was a big problem when Otis and his team were planning the elevators for the Empire State Building. It could take a long time for an elevator to get from the ground floor to the 102nd floor. It would take especially long if passengers were getting on and off at many different floors. The solution? Create groups of elevators called **banks** that only go to certain floors. The 68 passenger elevators Otis installed were divided into several banks. The elevators in Group A only went to the 7th floor. The Group B elevators went from the 7th floor to the 18th floor. Depending on what floor you wanted to reach, you might need to change elevators.

A motor like this raises and lowers the elevator with cables, or metal ropes.

HOW ELEVATORS WORK

The cross section below shows how most elevators work using a pulley. Strong metal cables attached to the elevator go around a pulley wheel. A motor turns the wheel, raising and lowering the elevator. A heavy weight on the other end of the cables helps the elevator go up and down.

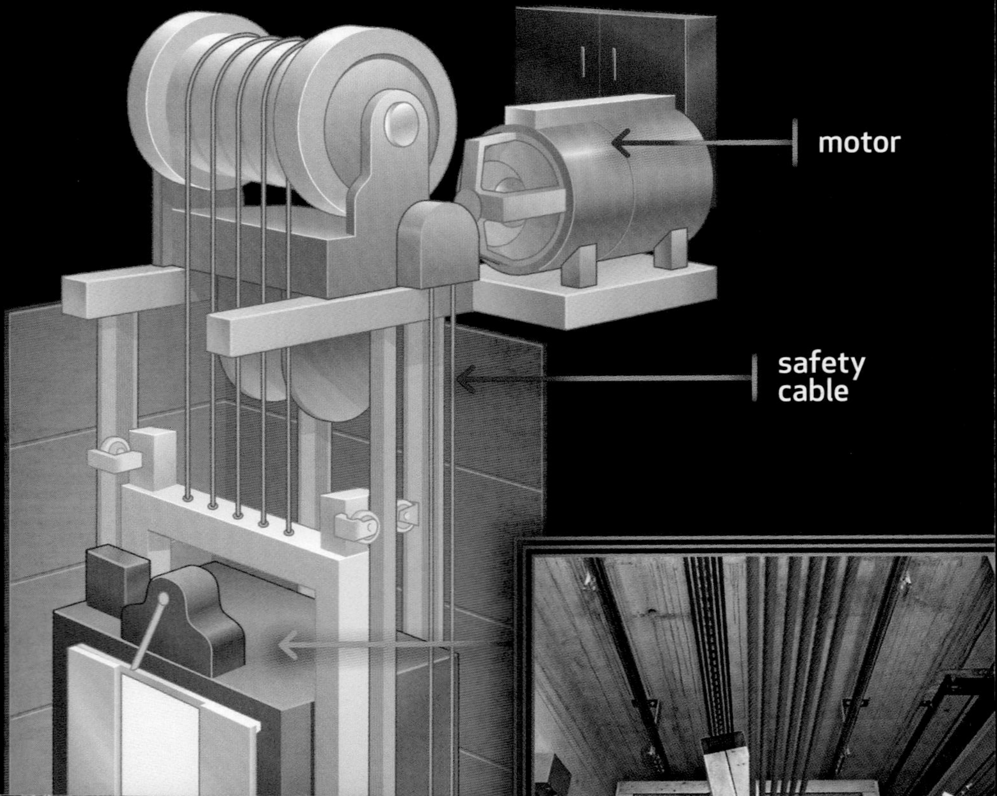

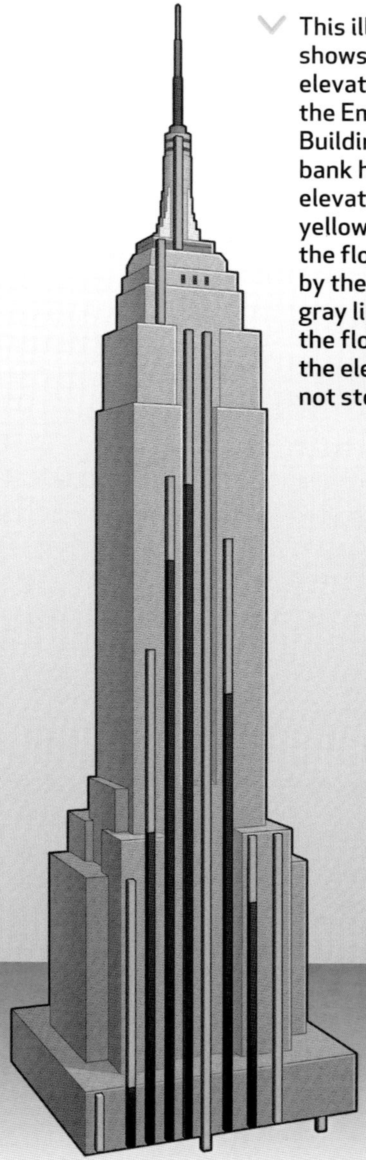

This illustration shows the different elevator banks in the Empire State Building. Each bank has several elevators. The yellow lines show the floors served by the bank. The gray lines show the floors where the elevators do not stop.

Heavy weights like these go downward to help cables pull the elevator up.

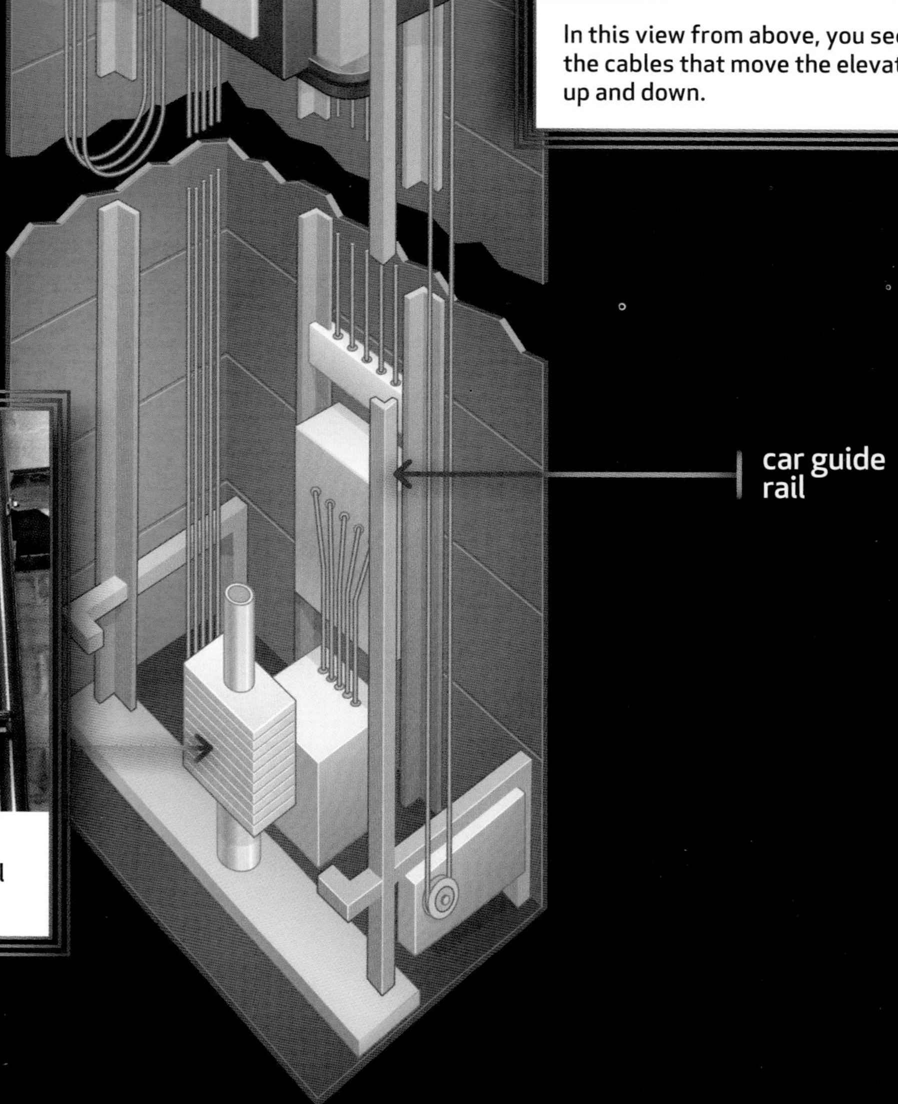

In this view from above, you see the cables that move the elevator up and down.

21ST-Century Elevators

Today, people enjoy riding elevators to the top of the Empire State Building to look out over New York City. Thanks to new technologies, the old elevators have been updated by the Otis Elevator Company to make sure they remain fast, safe, and comfortable.

These same new technologies have also been used to build a variety of amazing elevators around the world. For example, the Three Gorges ship elevator in China lifts boats that weigh up to 3,000 tons. It carries them over the Three Gorges Dam so they can continue on their way up or down the Yangtze River. The world's fastest elevator is the Taipei 101 elevator in Taiwan. The first Otis safety elevator traveled about 40 feet per minute, but the Taipei 101 moves 3,313 feet per minute! The CN Tower in Toronto, Canada, has the world's highest elevator with glass panels in the floor. From the top, riders can look straight down 1,136 feet. That's about the height of seven-and-a-half Statues of Liberty stacked on top of each other.

Elevators have changed quite a bit over the years. Can you imagine how different elevators might be 100 years from now?

Cars in this German factory are stored in tall glass structures. Workers use elevators to put cars in their slots and take them out.

A glass staircase wraps around a glass elevator in this New York City store.

Check In Why were people afraid to ride on elevators? How did Elisha Otis make elevators safer?

GENRE Reference Article

Read to find out about the well-known sights in New York City.

On Top of the

by Debbie Nevins

WELCOME to the 86th floor of the Empire State Building. This is the main **observation deck**. You can see everything from inside this glassed-in room. Or you can step out to the open-air walkway. It wraps around the whole building, so you can look out from all sides.

You're in the heart of Manhattan Island. It is the most famous of New York City's five boroughs, or sections. From this height, you can see many of New York's famous landmarks. Just use the **binocular viewers**. In fact, on a clear day like today, you can even see the states of New Jersey, Connecticut, Massachusetts, and Pennsylvania.

Later, we can go up to the 102nd-floor deck. From there, you'll see even farther, from almost a quarter of a mile up in the sky. There are 103 floors in the Empire State Building. The 103rd floor is almost at the top of the tower. It is packed with cable and other radio and television equipment. Visitors are not allowed—and that includes you.

WORLD

This is the open-air walkway on the 86th floor of the Empire State Building. Visitors can take photos of the city from here.

NORTH VIEW

CENTRAL PARK is a beautiful place to escape the hustle and bustle of the city. It was the first public park in the United States. It is more than 150 years old. The park has 843 acres of trails, lawns, ponds, and woods. It has 21 playgrounds, 36 bridges, two skating rinks, swimming pools, a carousel, a castle, and even a zoo, all in the middle of New York City.

THE EAST RIVER separates Manhattan Island from the boroughs of Brooklyn and Queens. Seven car bridges and one railroad bridge span the river. Thirteen car, subway, and railroad tunnels pass under the river.

QUEENSBORO BRIDGE

Manhattan is sandwiched between two rivers—the Hudson River to the west and the East River to the east. One bridge over the East River is the Queensboro Bridge. It connects Manhattan Island to the part of New York City known as Queens. Both the Hudson and East Rivers played an important role in making New York the world-class city it is. Before planes and trucks, goods shipped from all over the world made their way by boat up and down these rivers. New York City quickly became the center of buying and selling goods on the East Coast.

NORTHEAST VIEW

RADIO CITY MUSIC HALL is the world's biggest indoor theater. Over the years it has been a popular tourist attraction and a great theater to see concerts, movies, stage shows, and other events. In recent years, Radio City Music Hall has specialized in popular music performances. Located in Rockefeller Center, Radio City Music Hall's biggest attraction just may be its beautiful design.

GRAND CENTRAL TERMINAL

is certainly a grand building in size and beauty. After 100 years of trains coming and going, it might not be the busiest train station in the United States anymore, but it's still the biggest. In fact, there are more train platforms in Grand Central Terminal than in any other train station on Earth.

THE CHRYSLER BUILDING is one of the most familiar skyscrapers in the New York City skyline. A shiny, pointed crown of arches decorates the top of the building. Built in 1930, it is a perfect example of a style called Art Deco that was popular at the time. The Art Deco style was known for its smoothly flowing lines, its sharp angles, and ornaments such as triangles and rolled up scrolls.

SOUTH VIEW

FLATIRON BUILDING The unique triangle-shaped building called the Flatiron Building has fascinated artists and photographers since its construction in 1902. Why is it that shape? The Flatiron building had to fit in a wedge-shaped piece of land at Fifth Avenue and Broadway. This 22-story, 285-foot-tall building is only about six feet wide at its narrowest point.

Thank you for visiting the Empire State Building today. Did you know that the government made the Empire State Building a National Historic Landmark? That means it's one of the most important landmarks in the United States. In fact, it's an American wonder.

STATUE OF LIBERTY A small island in New York Harbor is home to the Statue of Liberty. "Lady Liberty," as the statue is also known, is a welcoming site to incoming ships. "Liberty Enlightening the World" (her real name) was a gift from France in 1886. She provides tourists with a great view of New York City from the observation deck in her crown.

ONE WORLD TRADE CENTER, OR FREEDOM TOWER

Completed in 2013, One World Trade Center soars where the World Trade Center, or "Twin Towers," once stood. The Twin Towers were New York's tallest buildings until a terrorist attack on September 11, 2001, destroyed them. The new One World Trade Center, or Freedom Tower, rises 1,776 feet. Sound familiar? 1776 was the year America declared its independence. At that height, One World Trade Center is the tallest building in the United States.

Check In Describe some of the famous sights that people can see from the observation deck.

GENRE Photo Essay

Read to find out about the movies that have featured the Empire State Building.

Empire State Goes

by Debbie Nevins

THE EMPIRE STATE BUILDING IS A MOVIE STAR! IT HAS APPEARED IN MORE THAN 250 MOVIES OVER THE YEARS. HERE ARE JUST A FEW YOU MIGHT HAVE SEEN.

In *Percy Jackson and the Olympians: The Lightning Thief* (2010), Percy Jackson is a teenaged boy who discovers he is the son of a Greek god. Atop the Empire State Building, the king of the Greek gods, Zeus, accuses Percy of stealing the source of Zeus's power—a lightning bolt. Percy's **quest** to clear his name begins. This quest takes Percy to the lands of other Greek gods, only to find himself on top of the Empire State Building once more at the story's conclusion.

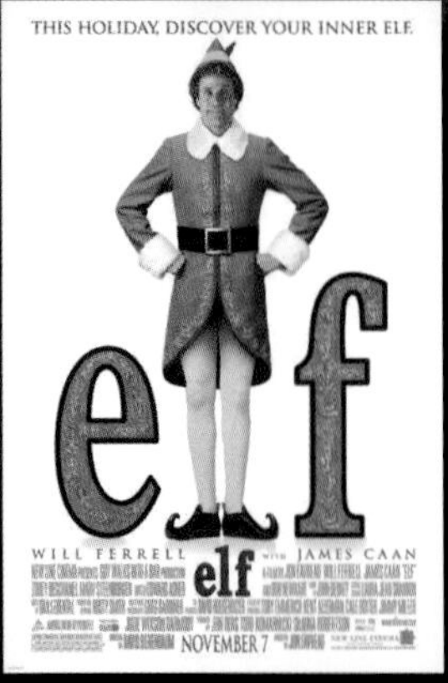

^ Actor Will Ferrell played Buddy the Elf.

In *Elf* (2003), Buddy the Elf travels to New York City at Christmastime. He is searching for his father. Buddy finds his father and goes with him to work at an office in the Empire State Building. Buddy is impressed by the tall ceiling and large metal plaque of the building's entrance. But you don't have to be an elf from the North Pole to know that the Empire State Building is special.

Hollywood

In June 2012, the Empire State Building lit up in red and blue to celebrate the movie *The Amazing Spider-Man*. Red and blue were chosen because they are the two colors on the suit Spider-Man wears. *The Amazing Spider-Man* was filmed in New York City. Viewers can spot the Empire State Building as Spider-Man swings through the city streets on the spider webbing that shoots from his wrists.

^ Logan Lerman starred as Percy Jackson in the 2010 movie *Percy Jackson and the Olympians: The Lightning Thief*.

The Empire State Building's most famous scene—the scene that made it a symbol for New York City and the United States—is in the movie *King Kong*.

King Kong meets his fate atop the Empire State Building in the 1933 movie, *King Kong*.

A group of people finds King Kong, a gigantic gorilla, on a faraway island. They capture him and bring him to New York City. He is to be **exhibited** as "the eighth wonder of the world." In the movie's famous final scene, King Kong escapes his kidnappers and climbs the Empire State Building in a panic.

The film came out in 1933, two years after the building was completed. It became a huge hit. Today, *King Kong* still has an effect on our culture. It was remade in 1976 and again in 2005. The dinosaur thriller *Jurassic Park* (1993) can thank *King Kong* for the idea of dinosaurs living on an island. King Kong has been seen on television advertisements for soft drinks and batteries. And the ape in the popular video game Donkey Kong resembles King Kong.

This is a scene from *King Kong*. Look closely. What's missing from the Empire State Building? The antenna wasn't added until 1950.

Check In In what way can a building be a character in a movie?

Discuss

1. What connections can you make among the four selections in this book? How do you think the selections are related?
2. What would it have been like to stand on the sidewalk in New York City in 1930, watching as workers constructed the Empire State Building? Based on descriptions from the selections, how would you feel about what you were seeing?
3. How have elevators changed the way people live and do business?
4. The Empire State Building is no longer the tallest skyscraper in the world. Why do you think it is still so popular among visitors to New York City?
5. What would you still like to know about the Empire State Building? How would you go about finding out more?